Beyond

Borders

Naomie Dieudonne

Villard & McCauley

ABOUT THE AUTHOR

Naomie Dieudonne is a freelance writer, poet, television host, and human rights activist. A woman with impeccable resilience and integrity, she has been praised by her peers. Naomie worries, all too often, most of us turn a deaf ear to what is plaguing minority communities, until the plight of injustice begins to affect our own lives. It is inequitable, Naomie asserts, reaping the benefits in the aftermath of struggle, while steadfastly remaining indifferent or ignorant in the fight for justice.

While Beyond Borders is a work of fiction, it challenges the broad spectrum of American ideals. It compels one to ascertain, even more broadly, how much of ourselves are we willing to sacrifice for others. And if "survival of the fittest" is the benchmark by which we measure the perpetual vigor of humanity, what happens when the most resourceful of us all stagger, facing endemic terror.

Beyond

Borders

A Social Exposition Through Short
Contemporary Fictions

Naomie Dieudonne

Beyond Borders is a work of fiction. Names, characters, places, and incidents, either are the product of the author's imagination or are used fictitiously. Any resemblance to actual persons, living or dead, events, or locales, is entirely coincidental.

For my sons,

Sebastian, Christopher, Raymarvens, and Rodney

You all are my source of strength and inspiration

And to my loving parents

Rev. Pastor Joel Andre and Lydie Dieudonne

We Stand

I have been the victim and witness

My tears and their tears mingled together with the sound of shame

We were the victims of rape

We were the victims of poverty

We were the victims of all kinds of sorrows

But we stood up

Yes, we stood up for our brave sons and daughters, for our sisters and friends

I am one of them

One of those women who cannot sleep at night

Yes, we stood up for our daughters, for our sisters and friends.

Tell Tale

– **Naomie Dieudonne**

CONTENTS

Naomie Dieudonne

2069	96
2068	97
2067	98
2066	99
2065	100
2064	101
2063	102
2062	103
2061	104
2060	105
2059	106
2058	107
2057	108
2056	109
2054	111
2053	112
2052	113
2051	114
2050	115
2049	116
2048	117
2047	118
2046	119

FOREWORD
By Jude Emmanuel

Sometimes we hear the voices in our heads. Every now and then, we hear them audibly. At worst, we don't hear them at all. Then suddenly, what we fear most, impales without warning. In Beyond Borders, Naomie Dieudonne's voice shouts like a staunch algorithm. And if at some point the storyline blurs, it makes one wonder, could it simply be a product of its grim reality. As "Equal Rights" doesn't necessarily equate to justice for all.

Most of us immigrants come from various shades, social backgrounds, and ideologies. And yet, what makes us different from one another, is precisely the bind that cultivates our "American" spirit. We are unique, in all sorts of ways. Yet, in our love for this land, we breathe as one. I gather, there aren't many sacrifices we have not, or will not shoulder, for where most of us call *home*. We take pride in carrying our fair share of the burden. Which brings me to this point: It isn't really imperative to lose our identity in order to have impact. We can assimilate through one another's pain. We need to be humans foremost, then we can hear each one's voice. Blinders aren't innate. And if somehow by my lack of sound judgment they happen to be, let us not indulge in their venomous landscape. We need to look beyond our own strength. Perhaps it will open our eyes more to one another's flaws. As such, Beyond Borders breathlessly explores matters that are endemic to all of us. Look closely at the pages, pay attention, as you will discover love, compassion, and not only what separates us, but what makes us *one*. After all, as humans, shouldn't we be one another's keeper? Beyond a shield of activism, Naomie Dieudonne narrates what makes her more than solely — an immigrant.

Fog

And

Fire

FOG AND FIRE

ONE

Inside the barrack align the shadows of dreamers. So much has changed. The world isn't what it once was. Not much is needed to end it all. Life is now years and memories wasted, hoping there is a *God* to bring them back to life. It's been three years since the war started, many hearts here are growing weary. Vasquez, the platoon leader, hands Angel a cigar and asks if he has ever played the guitar. Angel draws in a few puffs and starts to sing again. He wonders what has happened to Enoch. In these fields, unlike the Northern Alliance, which has traded in friends for favors, loyalty has become far more a virtue than being battle-tested.

Vasquez's cheek pulls back with a slight grin when he's reminded Angel was born on 9/11. Angel removes a picture out of his tattered uniform, cobbled together in cold sweat. As far back as he can remember, the dream never foreshadowed the rigor of the frontlines. Angel, along with the cavalcade of dreamers, simply wanted to make their country proud. The sound echoes like thunder in the night. The ground shakes. No one knows if they'll live to see another day.

Three years prior, Capitol Hill, Washington D.C.

"My name is Panama Jean-Baptiste. I'm an immigrant. However, this is now my home. I come from a long line of slaves who have fought for this land. Even to this day we have not completely conquered wars. We are merely counting days until the worst comes. Too many oppressed hearts have fallen to the grave. Too many soldiers have sacrificed their blood. Who is *king* today? Few can tell. America, in your gallant endeavor to free all, you've surely been betrayed. The cost of such freedom, which you've so eagerly promulgated, has caused you to suffer nurturing pains and tears. Yet, could it be in an attempt to renege on "Justice for all," you've blindly chosen to desert those who pride themselves as being of your own.

So, tell me, how hopeful are we today, knowing the blood and sweat of so many who have helped build, and made this great nation the home of the free and land of the brave, have been compromised by policies of indignation."

Brooklyn, New York

More than a few teardrops trickled down Abu's face, watching Panama bow to his knees after addressing Congress. Days earlier, the president had declared war on those who took refuge where freedom once abounded. They are all crowded in a basement. It's been a month already since mass deportations of undocumented immigrants began.

Abu sits idly in the dark. He glances at the ceiling, looks down, and exhales a few breaths. Lita cracks open the door to the only bedroom in the basement. She peeks out and notices three more men with their heads and knees to the ground. She had fallen asleep and didn't realize Faraji had brought more of them down. Lita looks over at Abu, slumped in his seat, the same position he's held since they finished breakfast. Panama will soon come home after picking up Enoch from school. Lita cannot wait until they get back. She wishes Faraji wouldn't, however. After another heated debate over the president's order, Lita is not too sure Faraji can really be trusted not to report them to Immigration Police. Panama has assured everyone, while Faraji thinks the president was justified in his actions, Faraji is nonetheless sympathetic to their cause.

There's a knock at the door. The three men get up and rush into the crawlspace behind the stairs. Lita runs out of the room in panic. She cradles her belly with both hands, her chest jerking with every breath. "Go back," Abu whispers, raising his arm while waving his fingers. He takes out the cell phone from his pocket. There aren't any text messages. It's been a week since the video monitor out in the front porch has not worked. Panama was supposed to take a look at it or have Faraji repair what both men think has been caused by the latest snowstorm. However, they worry about meddling neighbors. Ditmas Avenue isn't what it used to be. The neighborhood has changed quite a bit within the last few years. No one knows whom to trust.

Abu makes it up the steps. The knock on the door gets even louder. Abu is careful with each step, going through the living room. When he gets near the bay window overlooking the front patio, he kneels down, pushes the maroon, satin curtain aside, and raises his head just above the window seal. There are two uniformed police officers standing outside of the doorway. Abu's heart is racing. Why would the police show up at the house close to the middle of the day, he's thinking. As Abu looks on, Panama and Enoch pull into the driveway just as the two officers are about to leave. One officer walks over to Panama, while the other one stands with his back against the police cruiser. Panama chats briefly with the officer who had approached him, and they exchange a few laughs. The officer is a light-skinned male, with arms that look like tree barks. Abu drops his shoulders, looking out the window, breathing a sigh of relief.

Once inside, Panama brings more bad news. It is far worse than the death threats he has been receiving, which prompted him to alert Ryan, the Caucasian looking officer who had stopped by to check up on him. Panama is infuriated that neither Lita, nor any of the men seeking sanctuary at his house, has put on the news all day.

Lita is exhausted. She hasn't had a good night sleep in days. Although everyone tells her it's not healthy for her, nor the baby, she has barely touched the bowl of milk and cereal Abu has been trying to get her to eat all day. Most mornings, Lita munches on a small cup of oatmeal and stays without eating the rest of the day. When she hears the president has extended temporary protective status for women and children, a faint smile brims over her face. Yet just as quickly, her pale snicker fades when Panama tells her the new executive order is only extended to those whose children were already born in the U.S.; it will not cover women who are currently expecting.

Panama doesn't know what else to do. People have taken to the streets. Not a day goes by without an evening of angry protests. Panama recalls the former president's words during his farewell speech at the Rose Garden, "The sun shall rise again." America has since been under a cloud of darkness and uncertainty. Fear has settled in the hearts of the immigrant community, undocumented, and folks with legal status alike.

"What has happened to America?" "What has happened to this great nation I used to love?" Lita cries out

"I have faith in our government," Panama retorts.

"I refuse to believe that the government does not care about us."

It is close to the end of another cold night in Brooklyn. Soon, Faraji will come, enticing another round of arguments about—where has America gone wrong? Everyone is fearful of what will come next. Panama worries, with so many lawful immigrants hiding loved ones inside their homes, churches, and mosques, a war on all immigrants may soon follow.

"Who will be left standing in the land built with the blood of immigrants?" Panama shouts to himself as he prepares a cup of tea for the men in the room.

No one utters a word. Not even Abu. Panama knows how bitter Abu has become. He pats Abu on the shoulder and offers him a cup.

"Assalamu' alaikum," Panama greets the other men, as he also hands each one a cup.

They all begin to laugh. Panama doesn't know their names. He immediately agreed to have Faraji bring them over once he found out they were Abu's friends. All five men sit in a circle. Lita has gone upstairs to help Enoch with his Spanish homework. While she and Enoch are only a few years apart, he thinks the world of her. Yet, Enoch is upset with Lita for not eating adequately to help care for her baby. There must be a way for Lita to get help, he tells her. Lita is afraid she'll get locked up in a holding cell until immigration officials deport her. She asks Enoch about his mom. He doesn't say much. He simply looks at Lita with a ghostly stare. She knows it must still hurt. That kind of pain never goes away.

TWO

It's getting late in the evening. Finally, Faraji calls. He complains the streets in Brooklyn are not safe. He won't be able to make it. He urges Panama and the rest of the men to turn on the television. Lita screams out in shock as she starts to watch. Panama and Abu press her to grab something to eat and go to bed. The men, as well, are in utter dismay at the escalating violence permeating the streets. Scores of neighborhoods are up in flames. Some of the riots are getting more forceful by the day.

"The police have used commendable restraint thus far," one of the news anchors asserts.

"I think it is about that time for Martial Law," another one counters.

The men all sit without a sound but the television screen filling the room. Panama quietly bids a good night to the other men, bowing his head.

Panama has seen the good and worst of America, since he and his family immigrated to the U.S. more than two decades ago. He cannot fathom the loathing toward certain immigrants, which has threatened to rip America apart. Perhaps it shouldn't be such a surprise. The cracks of freedom in Lady Liberty may have started years earlier, the day of doom. It was hard for Panama to watch the destruction amid the fog.

That early morning, Panama sat behind the desk at the television station in utter disbelief. Hours earlier, he and his wife had gotten the much anticipated call before leaving for work. Panama's wife had just become an aunt for the first time. At 6:45 am, September 11, 2001, her only sister delivered Angel, a boy, and first child. Certainly, it was thrilling news. Two hours later, everything changed.

As everyone's eyes were glued to the large screen television in the lobby, "Oh my goodness!" one of the news editors yelled out, with both hands covering her face. America was under siege. The North Tower of the World Trade Center, the financial district of the world, had been struck by an aircraft. About fifteen minutes later, a second aircraft crashed into the South Tower. It was being reported, even the Pentagon had been rammed into by an airplane. As additional camera crews and news anchors were rushing out of the building to cover the story, both towers had collapsed. New York City was like a war zone. The streets along the West Side Highway were scattered with debris, raining dust. Convoys of NYPD Blue and firefighters had gone in the towers. Most of them didn't make it out.

Watching the Twin Towers crumble, so many eyes in the lobby were pouring out tears. Panama was familiar with the towering structures. He and Faraji were both attending school at a Lower Manhattan community college, blocks away. As calls were flooding the phone lines behind the desk, all Panama could think about was his wife. She was working as a housekeeper at the North Tower. Panama was getting restless. Hours had passed without a word from his wife. The terror emitting from the television became soundless at one point. When the North Tower had finally collapsed into a heap of rubble,

Panama said a quick prayer, hoping his wife had made it out on time.

By evening time, Panama sensed the worst had happened. The gut-wrenching thud in his stomach wouldn't let him rest. He put his head down and slammed his fists on the desk. The entire city was shut down and in a state of panic. Panama had no choice but to remain at work. When he finally got in contact with someone regarding his wife, it was Faraji. Both men were in tears on the phone. Faraji's wife, who also worked as a house keeper at the North Tower, had not called. That morning, Panama's wife left him with a peck on the lips and her usual pat on the cheek. They had planned on visiting her newborn nephew after work. It was the last words they spoke. The initial uneasiness of hearts had turned into utter gloom. Panama and his wife had just recently celebrated their second year wedding anniversary. She never made it home that night, neither did Sage, Faraji's wife.

It was such a strange twist of fate. Panama had asked to be reassigned to the World Trade Center, where he once worked as a security officer. The security agency he worked for had contracts with various businesses at the Twin Towers. Several men and women who were working for the agency had fallen victim to the horrific tragedy. Panama's wife had gotten him to change his mind about returning to work at the World Trade Center. Especially after Panama told her about the incident that took place years earlier. In 1993, when the North Tower was initially attacked by terrorists, Panama got his first job working at the World Trade Center. He'd told his wife how terrified he was once night, looking out the lofty windows, as he admired the breathtaking view of the city from above. Suddenly, he felt a cold chill. Panama later fell asleep and had a strange dream. There were sheets of dark clouds over the city, and yet its lights couldn't be tamed.

Oddly, the evening before the towers fell, after leaving school, Panama walked through one of the towers on his way to the train station to get his wife a gift from her favorite beauty store. Panama felt the same eerie feeling he had felt while working at one of the Towers. Panic had settled in his heart.

THREE

Lita is not feeling well. She has to get to a hospital. Things aren't like how they used to be. She worries if she's not careful, the baby may be taken away. So much has happened, too fast, too soon; everything appears to be a smog of shadows. Regardless of what Panama has assured her, Lita is comfortable where she's at. Brooklyn is safe, Lita tells Panama. She can't be around any men. Not after she had been forced to spread her legs. Though it burned, she sang loudly. It was a modest ruse to get everyone's attention. They all pretended not to hear. They had no idea a crime was being committed in that office, everyone claimed. Some had even dared to criticize Lita for merely rushing out with hush and small tears. Five years of packing groceries at the produce place, now it has come to this.

Dr. Armando will visit Lita today. Perhaps she'll persuade Lita to come to the clinic. All week, Dr. Armando has been telling Panama the baby needs care. After immigration officials practically ransacked the medical center a couple of weeks ago, Panama warns her no one can be too cautious. Dr. Armando reveals she has been receiving death threats as well. Although a devout Catholic, she sometimes wonders whether she's fighting God or evil spirits. Long ago, Dr. Armando and her parents crossed the border with great hopes and dreams. America is the land of paradise her parents would tell her. Dr. Armando knows things aren't the same for Lita. America is much different today.

It is the start of a new workweek. Things have been a lot calmer of late; the rioting has sucked a lot of people's energy. Panama has often complained; it's hopeless, fighting an army when there aren't enough legs to stand. It's all over the news, how exhausted the *Immigrants United* movement has been. Panama fears the weary walks will eventually lead to a slow death. Although there have been threats to bring in the National Guard, the governor is reluctant.

"They're pulling the rug from under our feet," Father Gabriel tells Panama, as the men convene at Panama's house. Father Gabriel has been at the forefront of the *Immigrants United* movement. Father Gabriel was one of the organizers who coordinated the "Immigrants for America" rally, which prompted a hearing in Congress. Panama, the three men he has provided shelter at his house, Abu, and Father Gabriel all converge in Panama's basement. The men are troubled Faraji has once again elected not to join them. Panama has not heard from him in days. And yet, he knows why. Panama is reluctant to tell the other men. It all goes back to what occurred at the World Trade Center. Faraji has felt betrayed by whom he once called "Blood Brothers."

"America cannot leave its door open for everyone," Faraji has told Panama in private. He worries his new family may fall victim to the same unappeasable hatred. Panama has not been so quick to pass judgement. After both men lost their wives to the dreadful carnage, Panama started distancing himself from his Middle Eastern neighbors in the neighborhood. He had heard somewhere that "Fear knows no boundaries," as such, to be audacious enough to insult a friend. It surprised Panama, when he noticed how nervous he would get around men or women whom he perceived harbored distaste in their hearts toward America. Abu's father was one of those men. When he, his wife, and five-year old son moved next door, Panama feared the worst. He had even contemplated moving out of the apartment. Panama and Abu's father, nonetheless, became good friends. Panama had observed how committed the family was, seeing Abu's father working nearly ten hour shifts at the car wash every day to provide for his family. Panama's wife had looked after Abu a few times.

Abu's parents, who had received "Temporary Protective Status" after overstaying their visas, have recently been deported as part of the president's mass deportation order as their *TPS* expired. Before graduating from high school, Abu dreamed of joining the military. He scoffs nowadays at the idea of forfeiting his life for what he feels is a government lacking the courage to defend those who would blindly sacrifice their blood for its honor.

"Both you and Faraji have had the same enemy turn its back on y'all," Panama has told Abu. Both men hate when Panama tots the line. Although Abu and Faraji admire his compassionate heart, they've accused Panama of being too lukewarm at times. Panama's response has always been to reassure the men—resentment has but itself as punishment. "That's Christian talk," Abu tells him. Panama is ever so quick to defend his faith. And yet, vengeance, he admits, can be interpreted through many lenses. He's told Abu and Faraji, if the heart can both love and hate all at once, the ultimate demise of human kind will be lack of empathy. Panama had seen many rejoicing around the world after the Towers had fallen. Faraji's wife, as well as Panama's wife's bodies, were never recovered.

"Who is King?" Panama argues. "Who's really winning this war when we've all suffered losses? If the only objective is to count and avenge specs of blood on one another's hands, and no one stands in the end, who wins, it is to what end?"

Crapshoot

....

Lita's condition isn't getting better. She has had the worst of luck. Lita traveled to the U.S. from Guatemala when she was twelve years old with an uncle she'd been living with. Lita has been on her own ever since her uncle got deported last year. Panama met her while working at the community center. Lita ran into the center, claiming her boyfriend had abused her. Panama sensed there was more to the story. He's never pressured her to tell. Lita has been living with Panama for the past month, wishing she hadn't gotten pregnant. Panama had asked one of the social workers at the community center to talk to her. However, Lita clammed up. He's even had a psychologist come to the house. Lita wouldn't speak. Dr. Armando is convinced it isn't Lita's boyfriend's baby. From the bits Lita has disclosed about herself, her mother died when she was six. She never knew her dad. Lita's uncle, her mom's brother, took her in after Lita's mother passed away. Her uncle, she says, who didn't have any kids of his own, paid a large sum of money so they could travel to the United States. He wanted Lita to have a better life. For the past week, Lita has been crying herself to sleep every night.

Junction Community Center, Brooklyn, New York

It's early February; close to three dozen men are scrambling around for answers. It is not good news. Father Gabriel has been murdered. He was shot in the back of the head earlier in the morning as he was getting in his car to attend a rally. There's an angry mob outside, threatening to set the city on fire. The mayor has been all over the news outlets appealing for calmness to prevail. The Police have not released a lot of information about the murder. Inside the community center, however, the men are incensed. Neither the DA, nor the mayor has returned their calls. Panama has asked the men, mostly leaders of the Immigrants United Movement to exercise restraint, yet no one seems to be listening.

Father Gabriel, a Haitian immigrant, had been a civil rights advocate and longstanding member of the Brooklyn's immigrant community. It has been more than two decades since he led the "Haitian Protest" over the Food and Drug Administration's HIV claim. A few years ago, when Father Gabriel began advocating for LGBT rights, the Church was in turmoil over what many believed to be—heretical sustenance. Father Gabriel squelched the upheaval with a message of compassion. Ignorance and loathing, he said, will always lead to bigotry, thus hinder the path of true wisdom. When Panama learned Father Gabriel was going to host a symposium on the impact of terrorism on race relations, Panama gathered most of his fellow students at the university where he was enrolled as a Social Work graduate student, and compelled them to attend. It was his first time meeting Father Gabriel. After the conference, Panama ran up the stage to shake Father Gabriel's hand. He had one question to ask, Panama told Father Gabriel.

"What makes a great leader?" Panama asked.

"Son, one who's not only willing or brave enough to die for a cause, but is wise enough to leave roots," Father Gabriel answered.

It's almost the end of the day. Panama sits alone in his office. Outside the door, there is anguish in the desolate shouts of angry men. The specks of rioters left on the streets have been attributed to the frigid weather. With the winter season about to end, there is no telling the type of chaos spring will unleash. Father Gabriel's gruesome murder has unsettled the hearts of many around the world and has left the Brooklyn immigrant community reeling with grief.

Faraji has picked up Enoch from school and will stay at the house until Panama returns.

In so many parts of Brooklyn, and surrounding Boroughs, tension is rising. Neighboring States are on the verge of declaring a State of Emergency. Police reports have been leaked. Two witnesses, it has been reported, saw a black male fleeing the scene after Father Gabriel had been shot. Another media source states, an additional witness claims to have seen two while males rushing into a minivan, with one holding what appeared to be a gun in his right hand.

As night falls, the streets are becoming, more and more, flooded with unease. The governor has affirmed she will not bring in the National Guard until it is deemed necessary. There are rallies taking place all over the United States. Even the Haitian government has lowered the flags at the National Palace in protest. At the U.S. Embassy in Haiti, the Haitian government has requested that its flags be flown Half Staff. Although there are diplomatic communications happening between Washington and the Haitian government, the president has not weighed in. Discontentment on the streets is at the highest it's been since the president's order for mass deportation.

At the house, Lita and Abu are watching the news with more than an edge of curiosity. Enoch sits alongside Faraji, on a wooden bench, pressed against the wall. The lower ground floor is as murky as the magniloquence of the pundits filling the room. Enoch fidgets in his seat every once and a while. His face has been buried in his cell phone, ruthlessly flicking the screen. He rests the phone on his lap, picks it up, and glances at it. Enoch has a worried look on his face. Faraji nudges him on the shoulder. For the past hour, he's been telling Enoch not to fuss; Panama will soon be home. There has been a surge in hate crimes of late, mostly against immigrants. The three men who have been at the house, all huddle in a corner. They mostly communicate among themselves.

There is something strange bothering Abu. He feels he has been hunkered down far too long. He can't resist the urge to join in the protest. Although his annoyance has a lot to do with him feeling like a caged animal, Abu is also irritated with Faraji's presence. Both men have Islamic roots, and yet their dislike of each other stems from different political views. The great difference in age, as well, doesn't help. Unlike Panama, Faraji sees Abu as wet behind the ears. Abu isn't at all impressed that Faraji, who's in his mid-forties, mentors young men at the community center. As far as Abu's concerned, Faraji's political views are as dubious as Panama's outlook of America. Panama, Abu asserts, is honest and forthright. Whereas Faraji, he believes, hides his true feelings behind a cloud of bitterness.

It's nearly a quarter past midnight. Panama has finally made it home. He goes to the basement; it's pitch-dark. Everyone appears to be fast asleep. Two other men who had dropped off Panama help him inspect the house. Once Panama tells them all is safe, the men leave. Upstairs, Faraji, who had elected to spend the night in a spare bedroom looks sound asleep. Although Panama had called ahead, letting Faraji and Enoch know he was on his way home, Enoch is awake. He runs to his dad as soon as Panama opens the door. No words are spoken. They simply wrap their arms around each other. Panama is thankful Faraji decided to stick around. He knew he had made the right choice in making Faraji, Enoch's godfather. There are some who weren't that thrilled with that decision. A few family members had complained about Faraji being Panama's best man at his wedding. Panama's family though of Faraji as an outsider. After what the two men experienced on 9/11, however, they have developed an infinite bond.

Being a single dad, it hasn't been easy raising Enoch. If not for Panama's parents and Faraji, taking care of Enoch would've been hell. Faraji has helped to — weather-the-storms. And so, Panama hasn't had to do it all on his own. Both men had remarried; yet both marriages ended in a divorce. Faraji at least has a girlfriend he sees on occasions and soon plans on them building a family. Enoch has had a lot of issues with the women his father brings home. He often runs them out with his insolent temperament. Panama, on the other hand, thinks Enoch is simply misunderstood. He was only nine months old when his mother died. Amid all the chaos and fear following the World Trade terror attacks, Panama doubted he and Enoch would survive another day. Panama had wept for days, weeks, and years. He's just recently learned how to cope. He knows Enoch is still hurting. He has received counseling, and yet, Enoch lives with haunting memories of stories told, which sting the heart.

In a year, he will graduate from high school. Enoch has thought about joining the Marine Corps. Panama doesn't mind the idea. As a matter of fact, many in the family have already joined the military. On Panama's father's side of the family, he has three cousins in the navy, and four more who have joined the army. Uncle Gilbert, Panama's mother's youngest brother, died in combat during the Gulf War. While somewhat delighted, at any other time, Panama would have been a little more ecstatic that his son has chosen to follow in the footsteps of what has become a family tradition. Panama, however, thinks wholeheartedly about his father's opposition to Enoch joining the military. It would be admirable to have his grandson wear the badge of honor of having served and defend his country, Panama's father tells him. Yet, he also at times wonders, how does America really feel about his nieces and nephews risking their lives, defending a country willing to reject those who share in their bloodlines.

Panama understands why his father has such a pessimistic outlook. Getro, another one of Panama's cousins, had fled to the United States amid political unrest in Haiti. Their Visas no longer valid, Getro, his wife, and four-year old daughter are now living illegally in the U.S., ever since the government's refusal to renew temporary protective status for undocumented immigrants. While Getro and his family have sought refuge in the U.S., fearing for their lives, Faraji isn't fully convinced the president's decision isn't unwarranted. He thinks such a ruling is solely to keep America safe. The heart of a preemptive government, he says, must be made of steel. Of course, this sort of thinking is the reason why Panama's family isn't so enamored with Faraji. Panama's parents have called Faraji "a hypocrite," even suggesting he is unhinged.

Faraji, having the luxury of being called an American Citizen, Panama's father stresses, is simply a result of well-timed luck. After Faraji's grandparents fled the Middle East in the late '80s, they were granted political asylum. There are thousands more, to this day, Panama's father tells Faraji, who are fleeing their homeland because of mass killings. Unlike Faraji, becoming an American citizen was a personal choice, Panama's father is quick to point out. Be that as it may, even as a naturalized citizen, Panama's father acknowledges there's enmity from those who do not believe he is truly an American. Panama's father doesn't get too wound-up at such assumption. He knows engaging in a debate over the idea would invite more animosity. What really matters, he says, is those who hold such a narrow-minded view must understand that immigrants have also fought to help America gain its freedom. And yet, this battle has never been about historical truth, Panama's father readily admits.

"There is unquestionably a fragment of America who will never accept us," Panama's father has affirmed. He hasn't forgotten the nauseating looks; the day he and his family immigrated to the U.S. Yet still, he feels at the core of the majority of Americans, there's love, decency, and profound admiration of immigrants. "I cannot fathom the America I know, ripping families apart at any cost," he has contended.

When Faraji told Panama's father, perhaps America shouldn't have opened its doors to certain immigrants, Panama's father reminded him it was Haitian soldiers who fought alongside Americans against the British, in the battle for Savanah in 1779, thinking Faraji's remark was a sly insult toward Haitian   Immigrants.

FOUR

Lita is bleeding badly. Dr. Armando has offered to drive her to the nearest hospital. There is still a heightened sense of alert all over the city. Lita is terrified. She's thinking the worst. Perhaps they'll keep her or possibly find out. She's grown to love the bundle of joy inside of her. Once in the emergency room, Dr. Alvarez and a few nurses rush over to Lita. She would rather have everyone think she only speaks Spanish. Dr. Armando knows it may not end well. In all likelihood, Lita might have miscarried.

"Lo siento, sé que he perdido a mi bebé," Lita places both hands on her stomach, her eyes full of tears.

"She knows," Dr. Armando tells Dr. Alvarez, who has alerted hospital registration staff. There are new rules in place ever since the government's health care law was revised. Lita doesn't have any identification. The new law requires the hospital to collect her fingerprints. Lita isn't comfortable with the idea. It was one of the reasons she was so reluctant to come to the hospital. Dr. Alvarez has been more than a colleague to Dr. Armando. They're blood relatives. Dr. Alvarez wants to help; yet she knows if she's not careful, she risks putting an end to her medical career, or even worse.

If Lita refuses to have her prints taken, one of the hospital's immigration agents will have to be summoned.

"State your name again, Madame?"

Dr. Armando holds on to Lita's hand and prompts her to say her name.

"Rosa Isabella," Lita holds her breath and nervously places her damp fingers over the screen. She takes the other hand and does the same thing. Yet again, she gently recoils her fingers.

"We have to do it again," the round face fella, with a heavy Caribbean accent tells her. Though he has tried several times, he can't seem to get a perfect print.

"I guess this will do," he bows his head while tracing the sign of the Cross, then clears his throat. His face is sweaty.

"Thank you, are you Catholic?" Dr. Armando reaches to grab his hand.

"Oui…Uh… I mean, yes, Madame," he shakes his head.

They get back to the house, Dr. Armando feels relieved, thinking about how terrifying the whole thing had been. She and Dr. Alvarez have put at risk everything they have worked so hard to achieve. It's even more revolting she feels, when other hands are stained in helping to carry the burden. She knows Dr. Alvarez feels terrible. The way this thing has played out of late, no one's conscience is beyond guilt. Panama has incessantly conveyed to Dr. Armando, in the fight for justice, martyrs aren't always willing victims. No one wants to violate the law, but what if it is unjust, Panama argues. How does one fight? What if there aren't other means to curtail judgement. Soon, Panama tells Dr. Armando, there might not be any gateways to America. Surely, everything has an end, Dr. Armando reasons. Yet at what cost?

Late in the evening, Dr. Armando sits at the edge of the bed. Lita lies on her stomach, her face is buried in a pillow, her arms curled up at the edges, firmly holding both ends. She hadn't really told anyone, before crying her heart out to Dr. Armando on their way back home. Dr. Armando can't help thinking about a foretelling adage she often used to hear about America back home.

"I remember the worried look on her face," Dr. Armando says of her grandmother. She'd told Dr. Armando, America is like an ocean. There are many small fishes swimming at the bottom, yet still they survive.

"One must never lose hope, she said; things will get better," Dr. Armando strokes Lita's back.

Panama and a group of Immigrants United leaders are planning for Father Gabriel's funeral. Alberta, a senior executive at a law firm, proposes an idea that has revitalized the spirit of the men in the room. She suggests a "Million Immigrants' March," in Washington, the day of the funeral. Abu, who's also present, advises that the funeral services be held in D.C.

"Let's bring the casket with us," Abu tells the group.

"Why should America bear the burden of one's ignorance?" Panama counters.

Abu is not at all pleased with Panama's response.

"I love you like a father, but your love for America blinds you," he tells Panama.

As the two argue back and forth, Jaclayhay, one of Abu's friends who has been staying at Panama's house with his brothers asks to speak. Although his English isn't perfect, Jaclayhay, the eldest of blood brothers, is much better at expressing himself than his siblings. He starts by telling everyone, while he and his brothers are grateful to be in America, they wish they hadn't come. "The lack of concern the world has towards our land has turned us into collateral damage," he says. His homeland, Jaclayhay admits, also shoulders the blame of failing to be one another's keeper.

As some of the men and women continue to argue, being asked to leave the country because you don't belong is nothing new, Panama's thinking.

When he and his parents first immigrated to the United States, Panama would come home from school every day crying. Some of his fellow students at school would tease him, telling Panama to "go back home." What angered Panama the most, those comments were coming from other black students. Panama's father wrote a note on a piece of paper and told Panama to show it to anyone who teased him again about going back to his country. Panama received more than a tease after he had handed the note to a classmate twice his size, which said, "Our ancestors boarded different ships." When the principal asked Panama's father what made him think it was appropriate to send his son to school with such incendiary note, "it is because of the incompetence of some of the public schools, failing to teach pertinent Black history," Panama's father answered.

"Most of us in here are Africans; we're one; let us unite as one," a woman shouts.

"Yes, we're one as immigrants, but I'm Latina," Alberta shouts back with a mocking grin.

Jaclayhay, with his rugged physique, and boyish look, walks over to Alberta and grabs her hand.

"You see, we wage wars against ourselves, because a lot more separates us than what's on the surface. Nevertheless, you're a lovely queen," Jaclayhay nips Alberta's hand with a gentle kiss. Panama laughs, bowing his head.

Ryan, who comes from a Jewish family, is an old college mate of Panama. He stops by along with a few community relations officers. Ryan is not indifferent to the grim and gloom of the plight of immigrants in America. He offers an historical perspective. Ryan recounts stories of the dreadful persecutions his grandparents had to endure in America.

"Are you saying we must keep hope alive? You sound like Dr. King," Jaclayhay mocks.

Fervent Journey

.....

As men, women, and children of all backgrounds are being mobilized for the immigrants' march, the government is feeling the pressure. More than six million undocumented immigrants have been deported; just about half of the people the government reckons to have *illegal* status, and already, a great number of State legislatures are up in arms over the overwhelming financial burden. The Federal Government, which had been subsidizing the mass deportations by levying taxes on some charitable corporations and refugee unions, has had to reintegrate funding to sanctuary States. Small businesses have shouldered most of the fiscal distress. Revenues are on a catastrophic decline, as these businesses have had to pay higher wages for positions that were previously filled by undocumented immigrants.

Wall Street, as well, has not reacted favorably to the volatile employment curvature. States budgets have suffered immensely throughout the U.S. The retail market has plummeted, as economists predict a massive recession if Congress does not take action.

With massive cuts in employment and protests over higher wages, some States have announced they will have no choice but to temporarily suspend their immigrant deportation program. Close advisers to the president, the media has reported, have warned him the declining economy may lead to a total collapse.

At Panama's house, Jaclayhay and his brothers are rejoicing. Lita is in bed with tears flooding her eyes. New York is one of the States which has indefinitely suspended mass deportation of undocumented immigrants. The news is all over television screens in America. Immigrants United leaders have advised those living in the U.S. illegally to employ cautious optimism.

"Though I knew my love for America was not in vain, it is not over yet," Panama is heard on the radio, speaking at a press conference.

"We were content being exploited, getting paid minimum wage," says Abu, who is not so excited about the news.

"This is a new America, Allah is good," Jaclayhay tells   him.

Hearts on Washington

.....

Crowds have gathered on Capitol Hill to take part in the historic march. The president has signed an executive order, essentially ending mass deportations. People have come by busloads from all over. Businesses are shut down in several States. There are members of Congress and even a few former presidents in attendance. Father Gabriel's body didn't make it to the Hill. His family has sent an empty casket, which lays bare adjoining the steps of Capitol Hill, surrounded by thousands. The police have yet to find out who killed him.

Lita, Dr. Armando, Jaclayhay, his brothers, along with Dr. Alvarez and Faraji have front row seats. Enoch and Panama's parents are all sitting a few feet behind Panama. Abu chose not to attend. The United Immigrant Council has elected Panama as Keynote speaker. The event is being broadcasted all over the world.

America, I have decided to write you a poem.

I love you

I've loved you since I first laid eyes on you.

Your glistening, although not always

immaculate beauty, is the envy of the world

When some of us dared to dream being in between

your bosom, it was indeed because of your

splendor.

While there are those who have labeled you a

scarlet woman,

we came to you for motherly love.

When a woman has been betrayed, surely, her

heart becomes cynical and intolerant in wanting

to love again

While we understand it may ease your mind to

secure your borders,

we, too, are your sons and daughters.

While some of us are perhaps the offspring of

adversaries, who have done you wrong,

others have bled with you while you've nursed

them.

We've felt your pain.

You've already shattered the hearts of so many,

waiting to be adopted by your loving hands.

Now, here we are, the ones you have rejected,

unesteemed as your own.

Here we are; we'll stand with you till the *End*

Don't allow an army of us to get washed away

by the violent waves of the ocean.

As you might have already realized,

It may serve you more favorably to have us

aboard the ship, in order for all to survive.

One week after the speech, the streets are once again filled with utter chaos. There has been what appears to be coordinated terror attacks in Europe and America. No one has claimed responsibility. The Pentagon and the White House are in an uproar over the attacks. The United Nations and NATO are scrambling for answers. There is so much terror on the streets; the president has imposed Martial Law.

Panama is in the living room, slouched on the couch. Enoch is sitting across from him, speechless, with his head down.

"We're going to war again, ain't we, Daddy?"

"I'm terrified…"

Passport

Tattooed

PASSPORT TATTOOED

ONE

Itold my parents I will not be going to college. "I'm leaving," I told them. They're both upset. Dad gave me a long speech about how much money he has spent on me. It has all gone to waste he says. As if he wants me to pay it back. "You're going to ruin our lives," Mom incessantly hollers. What about *my* life, I tell her. Today, I finally graduated from high school. I couldn't wait. I've had this dream ever since I was a little girl. When my friends were having boy crazy crushes, I was thinking about Paris. When they were dreaming about marrying a prince, I was still thinking about Paris. Not to someday meet my prince. I have daydreams of late-night walks near the

Eiffel Tower. "Wouldn't it be nice to have a handsome guy there with you," Skyler asked. She's like a sister. I'm an only child; she keeps me sane. Anyhow, "Who wouldn't," I told her. I would love to get married in France, if not England, or perhaps in some exotic island in the Caribbean. But not now. If I do get a chance to visit any of these places, I don't plan on staying too long. My dream is to travel the world. Skyler thinks I'm weird. I already know I am. I'm just waiting for the world to show me how crazy I can get.

Tribeca, New York

It's time. Tomorrow, I'm packing my bags, and I will be gone. I'm not sure where I will land. I have no money. At least not what I expected to have by now after saving every dime and penny I had earned working at the bike shop. Although Mom and Dad are disappointed, they are still willing to empty out their bank accounts. I told them not to. They've been crying all week. I will miss them. I have no idea how long I will be gone. I miss Skyler already. I'm sad, yet I don't want anyone to know. I need to do this for me. My pillow has been soaked with tears since I told my parents I was leaving. Even the doll collecting dust on my dresser looks unhappy.

June 23rd,

"Sweet dreams, Madison," Mom is crying.

"Sweet dreams, Mom."

I can hear Dad's sniffles in my room. He's stubborn. He won't come to me.

"Mom! Tell Dad I love him,"

I know she's still behind the door.

"Okay…Uh…Okay Sweetheart."

Her voice sounds funny; she's still crying.

"I love you, Mom."

She's not answering. If silence ever had a sound, this is it. Her shouts are all inside of me.

"Madison, please be careful. I love you and…I'm going to miss you," finally she lets out.

"Madison!" Mom storms in the room. She looks as if she's aged another twenty years. She hands me an envelope and holds on to me tightly. My throat twinges, sending a cold breeze down my belly. I'm feeling ill. Mom warms me. I can feel her heart racing. Her grip is damp. This is the last night we'll get to kiss each other good night for a while. I'm leaving early in the morning. Farewell New York City.

June 24th,

I'm up, however, I feel exhausted. It's been a long night, much like the worst sleep one can have. I felt like burying myself into the ground last night. I just want to be happy. I want to be free. Is it a sin, wanting to experience the world. Isn't that what life is about? Being young and free.

"Any beverages for you?" this cute flight attendant stares at me square in the eyes. *Oh shoot!* He must think I'm a freak. I bet my eyes are all red.

"Yes, I'll have a Coke."

Why does he keep staring?

"You said Coke?" He seems lost, as if he's undressing me with a naked eye.

Why? Is he nuts? This strange looking man is staring back. *Oh gosh,* he looks so familiar. He couldn't be, could he?

"Are you all right, Miss?"

"Yes, thank you." Go away!

Why didn't I ask for coffee? This thing tastes bitter. Why didn't I tell Mom and Dad the truth? I'm scared. I've been wanting to leave home for quite a while. And now I'm so afraid, running away. Who doesn't want to live dangerously? Certainly, it wasn't my wish initially. I'm on a flight to who knows where. I'm too young going through this. I feel guilty leaving home with so many secrets. I've never kept anything hidden from Skyler. There are things, however, you can't even tell your most trusted friend.

"Excuse me Miss, I know you. You're Pastor Gibbs' daughter, aren't you?"

"Yes, but I don't quite remember who you are, sir."

"It's okay, I'm Jeffery, Beatrice's father. Are you flying alone?"

I wish he would just go away. I'm already restless, trying to cope with so much on my mind.

"Yes, I'm traveling alone*," Please no more questions.*

"Y'all have family in London, I presume?"

I feel my head about to explode. "Yes," *Please go away.*

"Well alright then, I'll talk to you later."

Thank Goodness. *Oh No!* Why is he coming back?

"Hey, Madison, how long will you be staying in London?"

What the hell, I don't even know.

"I don't know, maybe a week or so."

"Okay then, enjoy the rest of your flight."

Thank God we only have an hour to go before we reach London according to the captain. I can't wait to see Josh. He was my first crush. It's sad how everything ended, especially after the racial debacle. Why couldn't I love whom I wanted to. It was so sickening of Dad, thinking Josh and I were so different. "Culturally distinct," were his exact words. I loved him. I still do, even though my heart has been ripped to pieces. No one could understand, not even Mom. I wanted so much to hate her. I think she knows. This is not just about Josh. Mom taught me everyone bleeds the same, and yet, things seemed to be different when Josh showed up. I'm dying to know what's so different about him. My head hurts.

London City Airport

I wonder if he'll remember me. It's been a year. I don't even know where Josh lives. Krystal says she'll help me surprise him. She and Josh have been friends for a long time. Krystal knows Josh and I aren't so worlds apart. Something strange is happening. I'm getting the chills. Krystal is late picking me up. Why does it feel as if I'm being followed?

"Skyler!" Beatrice's Dad shouts behind me.

"Jonathan?" this can't be real. My worst nightmare has followed me to London. I'm about to lose my mind. Who else was on this flight?

TWO

It's been another rough night. And now it's a lot harder not to look back. Krystal never showed up at the airport. I can't believe she would agree to take part in my parents' shenanigan. I'm starting to think Dad paid her off. It's going to make things worse now that Jonathan is here. My entire trip will be a living hell. It's all Skyler's fault, bringing him along. And Jeffrey — the creepy long beard man, that's how the kids used to call him during Sunday school, he'd been trying his best pretending not to be part of Daddy's cunning plan. Skyler has already spilled her guts. Dad made her promise not to tell. Who wouldn't betray their best friends for a trip around the world. It was only a small lie, Skyler admitted. I do not know what distresses me more, Jonathan being here or Mr. Lenard. They're both acting as if this is some sort of secret government mission. Jonathan looked so quirky with his dark shades and army fatigue. One would have thought I was being escorted to a witness protection program. Mom always thought of Mr. Lenard as an overly caring teddy bear who wouldn't hurt a fly. I find it hilarious Dad would send him to look after me.

I'm so angry. Then again, with Skyler being here, things will be less unsettling having her around. I just wish she hadn't told Jonathan. He likes me. It's hard to blame Skyler; Jonathan is her older brother. He's been trying to get me to return home. Jonathan is quick to remind me about my fairytale confession. It only lasted a week. Besides, that was before Josh came along. Jonathan is just as charming. However, he's much older and has had too many girls. I can't say I'm "head over heels" in love. I'm not quite sure what it feels like. Still, there must be a reason for me feeling this way. Josh's spirit lifted me up. He said I would have been his first. It was so tempting. He also would have been the first guy I shared my body with. Dad had to ruin everything. "He's not your type," Dad insisted.

Krystal and Josh are on their way to the hotel. I can't wait to give Krystal a piece of my mind. Once Skyler told her she and Jonathan were coming, Krystal should have warned me. I wonder how Josh feels about the whole thing. I'm surprised he's even willing to come. It's no secret by now, Daddy must have found out. Last night, amid all the chaos, I finally opened Mom's envelope. There's enough money in there to last me at least six months. I'm not planning much. It'll stretch up to a year. Mom and Dad knows I'm a simple girl. I'll probably save some of the cash as emergency funds, unlike Skyler, who without a doubt, would blow that bundle in makeup. Inside the envelope was also a credit card. There was something else. It nearly made me cry. It should have been expected, knowing Dad.

Sweetheart, I miss you already

You are my pride and Joy

Don't think you are old enough

You still have a lot to learn

I told your mother, nonetheless, this is a good time to start

I won't fuss, then again, I had to make sure you would be

safe at all times. You will soon find out

I'm sorry, well, not really

Love you, Dad

It is typical of Dad. He likes to rule with concealing authority and wealth. He and I often argue whether or not it is true love. Dad is from, what most would call, "Old money." Dad's great-grandfather made a lot of money as a real estate developer. By the time Dad came around, there was a shift in the family philosophy. It was geared more toward altruistic and pious ideals according to Dad. The Hansen family believed the most noble way to spread their wealth was to have a preacher in the family. I don't think Dad agreed. However, he didn't have a choice. Grandpa made him promise to attend Bible College. Dad had much rather been a mercenary entrepreneur. He has never been thrilled with me working. Dad was outraged, seeing his "Little

Princess" getting her hands dirty. That whole week, after starting work at the bike shop, was one of the few times I couldn't get the usual husky chuckle out of him. Seeing Dad so upset, I told him it would one day help me build an empire, handling money behind the register. It made Dad laugh. He was ecstatic to see his little girl being so self-driven. Yet it made me think about some of the crazy things people do for money.

Being so far away, it changes everything. Undoubtedly, it pains Daddy to have me so far out of his reach. Driving to the airport, our eyes traded empty stares through the rear-view mirror. I wonder what he was thinking. It was as if an invisible wedge had crippled our bond. Dad swore nothing would ever come between him and his little princess. Something has. And it's eating at us both.

Although I'm drowning in anticipation, waiting to see Josh, I'm beyond frightened. Whatever he and I had didn't end well. The first time Josh came over, I knew he wasn't welcomed by the look on Dad's face. Mom was overly responsive, trying her best to mask

Dad's discomfort. She and Dad thought Josh was born in Africa. I still recall the punch line, which wasn't at all funny. "I'll bet it doesn't snow like this in Nigeria, or Zimbabwe, or whatever part of Africa you're from," Dad rudely uttered with a smirk. I doubt Dad had even realized he was the only one in the room looking amused. As then, "Are you adopted?" He quickly followed with what has been the most humiliating day of my life. It was after Josh pulled out a picture of his family and showed it to Dad. A collective hush had taken over the room. Dad retired early, while Mom made cupcakes. Nevertheless, Josh's parents looking as milky as American pie, didn't seem to make much of a difference.

Josh thought it was fate that brought us together. He and his dad were visiting as part of a church conference last year. Josh's Dad is also a preacher. He said it's a never-ending battle, standing up for his son. Josh's dark olive skin seems to be the only thing that defines him. Dad has never admitted bias. Nonetheless, my walls have ears. "That sort of thing may be frowned upon," I overheard him telling

Mom. It had never been an issue, having been raised in the "melting pot" we call home, until Josh arrived.

I had pleaded with Dad to allow me to travel with the church missionaries on school breaks. He wouldn't let me. Some of the evangelists would bring back pictures of the boys and girls living in our orphanages. I always cry. Mom never wants me around when they are chatting about some of the horror stories of young girls being raped or sold for money. Boys, too, they say. I've told Mom, I would love to help. Certain parts of the world are not safe for young women to travel she said. I'm thankful to be in a place, much like home, where I feel safe.

Kindling Flames

....

There's a knock at the door. It must be Josh. Why does my chest feel as though it is being swamped by butterflies. Thank goodness no one else is here. Although Skyler and Jonathan are only a few doors away, I'm hoping to get some alone time with Josh before everyone invites themselves in. *Oh gosh*! I must look like a clown with all that makeup on. I'm going to kill Skyler. It was her silly idea.

"Just a minute, I'll be right with you. "

"Hi, Josh."

"Hello, Madison," he kisses me on the cheek.

"Where is Krystal?"

Without a doubt, he had to have noticed my inner blush. I don't remember him being so tall.

"She thought better of it. She'll be back later. You look beautiful."

"So do you," *Oh no! Blaaahh!*

"I look beautiful or handsome?" He laughs.

Why do I feel like I want to go back home. I didn't come here for him anyway. Okay, I did. Now what?

"Where is everyone?" Josh takes my hands and walks over to the couch.

"Probably eavesdropping behind the door. I told them I needed some privacy."

"I miss you, you know."

I hate it when he looks at me that way. I mean, his eyes slant, as if he's trying to seduce me with a not so modest gaze. I feel overwhelmed. Josh says, he and I are like white sand and seagrass, destined by the waves of the ocean. I'm not sure I understand what he means. The only thing I'm able to piece together for now, "That sort of thing" Dad claims many frown upon deepens over time.

THREE

Mom called. Not much was said. Just as I had expected, she didn't sound happy. It didn't take long before Dad took over. He was as stubborn as he's ever been, claiming if he had to do it all over again, he would send an army after me. It's unconscionable, he said, for a young woman to think she can travel the world on her own and be safe. Dad went on and on about being cautious of wolves in sheep's clothing. I hope he has enough money to fund his entire "private eye" team until we get back. I'm planning to tour Europe, then travel to the Caribbean. Afterward, who knows where I'll end up?

It felt a bit strange seeing Josh last night. Sort of like when you're sneaking to take something that's yours without your parents' approval. Skyler likes him a lot. I wish I could say the same for Jonathan. The whole thing is embarrassing, having chaperones around. Everybody went out sightseeing. I'm too tired. I told them I would stay back; there's so much on my mind.

"Okay! Okay! Who is it?" It's getting to be annoying. This is the fourth time. I hope it isn't that hotel clerk again. I told him he had the wrong room.

"Yes, this is she; can I help you?"

Oh, my goodness!

"Who are you? Please don't hurt me."

"No!"

I have no idea how we made it out of the lobby. There would have been hell to pay if I didn't agree to everything. I feel dizzy. My head is spinning. I want to scream. It was too scary to put up a fight. Now I'm thinking I should have. The car reeks of cigar.

I'm terrified. It's so dark in the back of the van. I wonder if anyone saw me. *Oh gosh! Why m*e?

I wish I knew why this is happening. I thought it might have been a prank, until that fat guy pointed the gun at me. I'm not sure where we're going. *Wait, we're stopping*?

"Get out!" the chubby guy yells.

"Where are we going?"

"Get up," he grabs my arm and picks me up.

"Please! Please don't hurt me. Where are you taking me?"

"Shut up and you won't get hurt," the older looking man shouts and gets in the back.

They're dragging me out.

"Stop! You're hurting me."

The older guy, who must have been the driver, has his hands around me. "Now get out!" He shoves the gun at my side. I'm scared, where is everybody? We're going into this house; the neighborhood looks creepy. There is hardly anyone on the streets. The building looks so old. Both men are at my side, squeezing the life out of me.

"Let her go up the steps first, Jack," says the fat guy.

"Please, don't hurt me. Where am I going?"

"Not one more word out of you," Jack squeezes the gun harder against my back.

It smells terrible in here. I hear what sounds like a young girl screaming. My throat is burning and itchy. My entire body is going numb. Jack (I hope that's his real name) has me locked up in a disgusting looking room. *Please Lord! Let this be a prank.* The room is virtually empty. There aren't any furniture; apart from what appears to be a twin size bed. The windows look as if they have been boarded up from outside. I can't stand the smell. Maybe it's the nasty looking rug by the door. I feel cold and naked. There is only one small bulb in the ceiling fan. The room looks hazy. Jack told me he would be back. I don't want him to. Who knows what they'll do to me. *Oh gosh!* This is a nightmare. I can't stop crying.

Maybe they know about Dad. He'll give them everything he has to get me back.

The fat guy is outside the door, shouting. I know that voice. I knew it was him. He must have followed us from the airport. He had asked where I was staying before Jeffrey rudely interrupted our conversation. He had to know I wasn't traveling alone. *My goodness!* How did they find me? Some girls are stomping their feet out in the hallway. I can't tell whether they're singing or crying. There are men. I hear lots of men. I don't even know what time of the day it is. *Oh Lord!* Someone's coming in.

"This is for you to eat," says a girl with long, straw-colored hair. A man with pale skin and golden hair trails behind.

"If you're done, get out," the man tells the blonde girl.

They cook in here? It looks like bean soup with rice. I'm not hungry.

"Here, try on these clothes and Jack will check you out in the morning," the man hands me a trash bag.

Check me out? What the hell does he mean?

"What's going on, sir? Is Jack here? Can I speak to Jack?"

He ignores me and shuts the door on his way out. I don't even know why I asked to speak to Jack. He hardly looks like someone who would hurt a fly. Perhaps he wants money. Why the girls? I hear so many of them. The plate of food is scorching hot on my lap. My hands are sweaty. I can't take this.

"Let me out! Please, let me go," I run towards the door.

The plate of food falls on the floor. My hands are shaky. I fall on my knees.

"Please, let me go!" I pound the floor with my hands.

"Can you shut the hell up?" the man with the golden hair shouts, peering into the room.

"Please, let me go! Take me back! Take me back!"

He charges toward me.

"You want a bloody nose?"

A dark-skinned girl runs after him. "Let me talk to her," she tells the man. She helps me up, rubs my hair, and sits next to me on the bed. The man tells her I better clean up my mess and leaves. The girl yells for someone to get a mop bucket. Two other girls rush in the room. The one pushing the mop bucket has tan skin and blue eyes. The other girl, a chubby blonde with curly silk hair, looks just like me. She bends down and wipes the hardwood floor with a rag. The girls tell me to keep quiet. The dark-skinned girl, Abigale, the other girls call her, gestures with her hand for them to leave after the blue-eyed, brown skinned girl, and the blonde with curly hair are done cleaning.

"Listen, it's best to keep quiet," says Abigale.

"What's your name?" she asks.

"Madison," I glance toward the door. "What is this place? what do they want from me?"

She gets up, closes the door, and sits back down. Abigale thinks I may be safe for now. She says she overheard Jack and the other men arguing about what to do with me. I'm not sure I can trust her. She gets me to smile, however, as Abigale notices my New York accent. I wonder if she's also from the

U.S.; neither Abigale, nor the other girls sound British. Then again, the same could be said of Jack and the fat guy.

"Okay, enough chatting," the golden-haired man walks back in the room.

"You have a goodnight, Madison," Abigale hugs me on her way out.

"Don't forget what you promised me," the man tells her. He then wraps his arms around Abigale's waist.

I don't know what to make of this place. Abigale was friendly, but who knows what's in it for her. The bed is nicely made. I rather sleep on the floor, however. I miss Mom and Dad. Where are Josh and Skyler? And why in the world did Jeffrey and Jonathan leave me behind. I can't believe they've let this happen. *Oh gosh!* It's all my fault. I should've gone with them. The floor is cold. I need to get back in bed. *Wait a minute, is that Jack?* Oh, my goodness, he's back. I didn't think I would see him until morning. Is he coming in?

"Hey Madison, why do you have the same clothes on, didn't Arc give you clothes to wear?"

It is Jack. What clothes? And how does he know my name? I knew I shouldn't have trusted Abigale.

"There she is," Jack tells this tall, bullish looking guy, with a suit and tie standing at the doorway.

"Good to meet you, Madison," he smiles.

For a moment, he looked like this man I had seen at the hotel. His grin is cold and terrifying.

"How old are you, Madison?" he asks.

"Eighteen,"

"You look much younger," he says.

He scares me. I take a quick glance toward Jack, who's staring back with a piercing tenacity in his eyes. Something tells me things are not about to get better. This is getting beyond petrifying. I'm afraid to show it. The tall guy wants to know what does Dad do for a living.

"He's a pastor," I tell him.

"C'mon now, Daddy's little girl; what does he really do?" He laughs.

"Now can you let me go, he'll pay you whatever you want," I say to him after admitting Dad also owns several corporate office buildings in New York.

"Good girl! A little princess with a rich daddy?" he blows me a kiss.

"What's happened to Jonathan and Skyler? Dad sent them with Mr. Leonard to look after me. How did you all know they weren't with me?"

"See you soon, Little Angel," the man with the suit answers, his voice full of sarcasm.

A warm breeze sifts inside my chest, then turns cool.

"All right, we'll be back in the morning," Jack nods and slams the door.

Things do not look good. It's going to take a miracle to make it out of here. There are hasty footsteps. Someone is coming in. It's Jack.

"What's your girlfriend's name again?" he asks.

"Who? Skyler? No! Don't hurt her Jack, don't hurt her,   please!"

FOUR

Everyone wears a face of terror when the man in the black suit comes in. He was here this morning. The rooms were soundless for once. None of the girls know his name, not even Abigale. All they've ever heard anyone call him is—Boss. His feared, perhaps, for holding everyone's lives in his hands. Jack doesn't say much when "Boss" is around. It's never a good time to fool around, Jack has told Abigale. Most of the girls seem to love Jack, nonetheless. More often than not, his pleasant, they say. Yet at times, spiteful craving engulfs his eyes. He's made them do some terrible things.

Jack has told the girls he doesn't hate women. "It's strictly business," he says. It's rather callous of him to think exploitation isn't hate. At first glance, one would think he's all charm. Jack has this weird thing he does with his eyes. They shift, before catching your attention with indecorous lust. You're locked in, if not careful. His voice reverberates, almost reassuring, until he gets angry. Jack looks like the prince on a horse most girls dream about. He had promised to marry one of the girls. That's how he got her to come. Her father is a surgeon. When he found out his sixteen-year-old daughter was dating an older man, he forbade her from seeing Jack. When the girl's father discovered Jack was still pursuing his daughter, he had Jack arrested for statutory rape. Jack still gets angry telling the story, according to Abigale. For a while, both he and the girl were on the run. No one knows what has happened to her after she "moved out."

There are no signs of God; yet all sorts of angels live in this place. Days and nights are filled with visitors, depending on who is awake or whose turn it is. I doubt any of the girls here really sleep. Men come from all over, seeking ecstasy on a warm bed.

What they delight in, however, burns the essence of heavenly souls.

The sun hardly shines in here. It's only been three days, and already, I've lost hope. Crying doesn't help. Shouting makes it even worse. I've slept, and cried, over and over again. It's far more sickening than I could have ever imagined, seeing and hearing things that constantly keep me up at night. The girls tell me I'm lucky "Boss" has not yet "Prized me up." I'm told he doesn't like to lose money. Abigale says Dad's wealth may have something to do with the delay in— sending me out to work. The longer the wait, she says, the less likely my chances of staying in the house. A girl, last year, waited just as long before she was sent to a different location. Abigale insists on me telling Jack I miss being with my boyfriend.

I was reluctant to ask; yet I'm glad to have inquired how come Abigale knows so much. She says I can trust her, as long as I'm willing to "play the game." Most girls aren't able to survive unless they play along, she says. It burns my stomach.

Everything in here gives me the creeps. There are five other girls in the house, sharing four rooms. The kitchen looks like an oversized closet with old appliances. The ceramic floor is constantly littered with cigarette butts. Surprisingly, the girls do a great job, always cleaning up. They take turn doing chores to keep sane. No one is allowed near the entrance door to the apartment, where Arc and another man rotate shifts, sitting on a stool. Along the long hallway leading to the lone bathroom in the back, the bedrooms line up opposite one another. Downstairs, where some of the "house pimps" live, there is a full and half bath, which the girls have to ask permission to use.

Although most of the girls have welcomed me as part of the sisterhood, I'm horrified. I don't belong here. I want to run. Part of me, nonetheless, feels guilty for wanting to escape. I miss home. I just want to go to sleep. The girls feel the same way. Especially Abigale. All she talks about is her younger sister, who's most likely by now enrolled at a university in New York. Abigale doesn't talk much about her parents. "It'll give me false hope," she says. Tears roll down her face talking about the graduations and birthdays she's missed. Abigale imagines herself every night in a cap and gown or sitting in a classroom where Criminal Law is being lectured.

Abigale wept with laughter when she found out I'm eighteen. It felt awkward, telling her I was solely here on vacation. But then, she made me feel less guilty by sharing how she ended up in the house of hell. It has been close to eight years. Abigale was getting ready for her first date with a guy she'd met at a bowling alley. The guy was much older, which made Abigale hesitant about telling her parents. He had invited her to go out to lunch and see a movie. As soon as Abigale had gotten off the bus to meet him, a van pulled up. Suddenly, she and two other girls were forced to get in the back of the van at gunpoint. Abigale moved to various states in the U.S. until she turned eighteen. She then flew out of the country with a man she called Uncle. Abigale had a chance to run. She was afraid they would catch her and beat her to death like they did to her friend who tried to escape.

She and the girls would love to return home, says Abigale. They feel a lot safer here, however. The girls don't have to worry about getting beat up. At least not by strange men. Some girls have gotten kidnapped, being on the streets or at a hotel, I'm told. Abigale has been with Jack for four years. She admits he allows her a lot more freedom than the other girls because he knows she won't be so quick to run away. Jack tells her, in a few years, she'll earn enough trust to be in charge of what he refers to as — his group home. Abigale doubts anyone back home would want her back. Everyone, including her parents, she says, may feel that she's "dirty."

FIVE

Another girl comes in. Her face is covered with dark powder and red lipstick. Her body looks brittle. No one knows how long she'll stay. She appears to be my age, maybe a year or two younger. She has on a sleeveless shirt and shorts that might as well be ladies undies. Arc says I'll have to give up my room. It's house protocol when a new girl moves in. No one really shares rooms, except for Abigale. She pretty much sleeps wherever she wants. Most nights, she prefers to stay downstairs with the men. Although she has her own room on the bottom floor, Abigale says she gets lonely. I have no idea where I'll be sleeping tonight. Arc tells me I'm bad for business. I wish I knew what he meant. Thank God Abigale won't let him put his hands on me.

Today makes it a week being here with the girls. Abigale thinks Jack and the boss are after far more than money. If she knows what it is, she's probably too afraid to tell me. She and Jack are close. However, Abigale won't go too far to cross him. I still can't wrap my head around what has happened. It's hard to trust anyone. I just want to get out of this place. I'm hoping we all do, soon. Not too many men showed up today. It has something to do with the new girl and how she was picked up. Abigale can always tell when the boss is upset with Jack. After the fat guy, Alex, and Jack dropped off the new girl this morning, Jack told Arc and the other two house pimps not to let anyone they didn't know come in. It gets that way sometimes, according to Abigale. But after a few days, it is business as usual.

It must feel like a nightmare for the new girl. I know what it's like to be isolated in that room. It felt as if I was inside a tomb that first night. She hasn't eaten much. She's been asleep for hours. The girls and I are gathered in one room. There aren't any televisions on our floor. We just sit and talk. One of the girls looks annoyed. Everyone calls her Erica; yet it isn't her real name. Abigale says that's how some of the girls cope. It feels so much better being part of a world of make-believe. Tina, the brown skinned girl with baby blue eyes, says she often forces herself to believe she's a character in a movie. "It's like pretending you're having a nightmare," says Sheena, the round face, blonde girl, who looks a lot like me. "But then," she adds, "you kind of get upset the dream has gone on too long."

"When will you get your turn, *Hoe*?" Erica snaps.

"Leave her alone," Abigale tells her.

"Yeah, leave her alone, Erica," Sheena chimes in.

"What are you guys, twins?" Marjorie teases after sipping from the *firewater* bottle in her hands.

Marjorie doesn't speak much. She takes another sip, lifts her head, and stares across the room as if looking through the wall. We're all sitting on the floor in a circle.

"I just don't want that bitch to think things are as hunky-dory for everybody in here," Erica shouts. "I'm just saying. This ain't some bougie' girl slumber party. I'm sitting here thinking it's going to be the first night in months I'm not going to get fucked against my will."

"Stop it! Erica, she knows this shit is real," Trina tells her.

"Let her vent; it's not you," says Abigale, while she hugs Erica.

Why does it feel like everybody is against me? I didn't ask to be here.

"Tell her; tell her, Abigale. She has no idea what we girls go through," Erica's head slumps above Abigale's shoulder.

"Let's not do this to her, girls. Everybody here is feeling the pain, one way or another," Marjorie utters, almost with a whisper. Her eyes look lifeless. She briskly tilts her head back, the bottle still within her lips. Erica's eyes are full of tears, staring at the ground. She then gets up without a word and heads toward the door. Abigale follows her and takes hold of Erica's hand; both girls wrap their arms around each other.

"She's tired. She doesn't want to do this anymore," Abigale's voice breaks.

The girls are used to it by now. They've each had their days. It makes me want to run. We all miss home. Marjorie says she came to London on a student visa. She reminds me so much of Josh, with her long, braided hair and dreamy eyes. A family friend had persuaded Marjorie's parents to have her study abroad. The friend promised her parents, who didn't have much money, that he would help care for Marjorie until she was done with school. Everything changed when she arrived four years ago. Marjorie never did go to school. Things were much different living with the family friend than she had imagined. He would throw weekend parties, inviting a lot of older men and young women to the house. At first, Marjorie didn't think nothing of it. Until one night, the family friend tried to get her to sleep with one of the men. Marjorie fought vehemently against doing that sort of thing. The family friend made her cook and clean, every day. He wouldn't allow Marjorie to speak to her parents. Later on, he told her if she didn't do what he wanted, he would have her parents executed.

"He ended up giving me a big belly," Marjorie says with an angry laughter. "I never agreed to do anything with him," she says.

When asked about the baby, Marjorie's face grows even more furious, yet sad. Her cheeks shiver as though about to explode. She doesn't want to talk about it.

"It started with one man," Marjorie says, "then the next, then the next, until I couldn't count. I never agreed to anything. I would never, never...uh...you understand?"

Abigale, Sheena, and I, all hug her.

"I have a story to tell, too," Trina shouts out, loudly.

We all start to laugh and cry at the same time.

"When you're done, it's my turn, Pretty Blue Eyes," Erica waltzes back in the room.

We begin to laugh all over again.

"Soon, you will all be back to work," Arc barks outside the door. A shrill silence floods the room.

Trina and Erica share similar stories. They were both kidnapped at gunpoint, walking home from school. They're both from foreign countries. Trina initially traveled to the U.S. with forged documents when she was sixteen. The first week she arrived, Trina was forced to "work" at a strip club. From then on, it wasn't long before she was out on the streets. Trina was once arrested for prostitution. She was too afraid to tell the police she had been kidnapped. It's been three years since Trina last saw her parents.

Erica has been in so many places, she hardly cares to remember. "My passport is tattooed," she says with a faint smile. Erica talks a lot about Jasmine, another girl she'd met. Jasmine was coerced into selling her body by a man she started chatting with on the web. He had promised to take her around the world. Jasmine ran away from home, fleeing physical abuse from her stepfather. But then, less than a year after she ran away to be with the man she had met on a social network site, Jasmin's body was found in a dumpster.

Erica admits, it is a difficult thing to forget. It takes a lot to fill that void she says. And yet, the smallest of things bring it out. She and Jasmine were like sisters.

"I've had the worst luck in life, or maybe not," Erica sighs, looking as though she lacks the strength to voice her pain.

"Do you think God will punish me for the baby?" Erica asks.

"What baby? You mean…uh…ok…uh," I'm at a loss for words.

"You should know, don't you? Didn't you say your dad is a pastor?"

"Ok ladies! Party is over," Arc interrupts.

Jack wants me to get ready. I'm scared. I start to bite my tongue. Marjorie offers me a sip. It'll calm my nerves, she says. I feel worse. It burns. My chest is starting to hurt. I can't breathe.

"Hurry up, Young Lady. The boss has a special one coming for you. It's finally your turn," Arc looks amused.

Oh no! It is me. I'm losing all my strength. The girls hug me. I can't stop crying.

"Please, Arc. No!"

"If you don't do what he says, he'll hurt you real bad," Abigale grabs me.

"Take her downstairs," Arc orders Abigale.

I   feel   as   if   I'm   about   to   faint.

A cry for help

....

"Madison Renee?" he rubs my hair.

"How…how do you know my name?"

He puts his hand over my lips and whispers in my ear. The alarm is going off. I hear lots of footsteps and people shouting.

"They're in here; they're in here," the man shouts through his walkie-talkie.

What a Relief! There must be more than a dozen officers in here.

At the police station, Mom and Dad both are holding on to me. Their eyes are bloodshot with tears. Daddy squeezes tighter and tighter. Jack and Alex tried to abduct Skyler. Josh and Jonathan followed them and alerted the police. The new girl at the house was working undercover.

"My Son! Thank you," Dad cuddles Josh.

"I'm sorry, we shouldn't have left you alone," Jeffery clutches my hands.

Tribeca, New York

About a year later

The sun is bright. Yet all I'm seeing are shadows. Erica, Marjorie, Trina, Abigale, and Sheena, all torment my mind at night. Abigale sounded so dejected. She called me, crying. She's about to have a baby. She worries, Jack may be the father. Abigale has her mom, nonetheless, for support. Her father died in a car crash a few months after Abigale was abducted. He had become addicted to the bottle.

Marjorie and Trina are both fearful about going back home. They said they would feel like strangers at home.

Sheena didn't get to finish her story. Nevertheless, I found out she's much younger than I thought. I'm happy she's back in school. Sheena says she sometimes misses Jack. It makes me cry even more.

And Erica, she's also reluctant about going back home. Dad has promised to go with any of the girls if and when they decide to go.

Josh has proposed. Dad insists we must first finish our undergraduate studies before tying the knot. Dad brought home pictures of missing children the other day. I nearly threw up. Josh and I plan on traveling the world after we're done with school. We're hoping to help rescue children who fall victim to human trafficking. Mom has already made it a church mission. She wants to help adult men and women, as well, she says.

40 DAYS
&
40 NIGHTS

40 DAYS & 40 NIGHTS

Have you ever wondered

what it would feel like to read someone's mind?

Perhaps it might frighten you.

Or maybe,

it would terrify others,

knowing you're able to read their darkest thoughts.

How then, could it not be miserly,

not easily blending in.

Naturally, in discerning the slightest thought,

the meekest posture,

there exists copious, imaginary delight.

Lacking strength of will,

gleeful narcissism might reign as king,

harvesting unkempt mysteries.

Peace! Flee rather.

For such a gift induces wrath,

mercilessly branded irremediable paranoia,

89

however misunderstood.

What if, in trying to master the universe,

your wings get clipped.

In an attempt to exhort, one gets knocked down.

What if,

in offering love, the heart is ripped to shreds.

One can only hope to make it through the night.

Live your life! Vainly uttered lips full of contempt.

What if you have, but Holiness says enough!

Dare you resist the prophetic script?

The bough, therefore fallen, surrendering might.

Out of an altering wind, birthed a new soul.

The flesh burns into ashes,

wondering, will the dry bones ever live?

What if one were born with such a gift?

Would it be the envy of many?

Or would its bitter taste make one wish the heart
was empty.

But then, there is Joshua's story.

He had been counting days since he was ten years old. At twenty, he thought for sure, God was going to take him away. When Joshua reached his thirties, God surely must have changed His mind about a man born with what is to most, a noble gift. And yet, the grim reality of discernment aptitude almost became a curse. Endowed with the ability to scrutinize even guarded thoughts, Joshua was about to conquer the world. He nearly did. He would have, if turning forty hadn't sneaked up like a thief in the night. When the grey hairs began to betray his gift and youthful years. The joy of life wasn't everlasting. The pace of which bliss began to decay could be described as precarious at best. Joshua found comfort under the disguise of synthetic, youthful vigor. Much maligned, many did not hesitate to reckon that moment in his life — the mid-life crisis years. How ironic he thought. Not even near what most consider the twilight of life, Joshua began to once again count the days. This time, the reckoning of life was marred by nostalgic memories. Unremitting grief inundated at the core. Was he a man of candor or generous enough? If he were to die, was life lived to the fullest? How would the years between birth and death be perceived through the lenses of eternity?

Joshua grappled with himself to find the answers. Until, he one day, stumbled on a box of poems he had written over the years. While his spontaneous discovery could not mend the past, it did, however, provide insight as to what life should be about.

Joshua discovered he had quite a story to tell. Whether he'd accumulated more than enough to spare, or had been altruistic toward others, merely offered a glimpse of life. A chest of quiet verses enshrined the true meaning of life. The hours, days, and years were but a coffer of malignant occurrences, concealed in a pandora's box.

AN ODYSSEY

It has been another profitable year for one of the
richest man in America. What is an added million to
a man worth billions? Nothing, I suppose, to those
who have amassed enormous wealth. To Joshua,
nonetheless, or "The Powerful Mr. Hansen," as he is
often revered by his harshest critics, grasping
prosperity is the essence of integrity. As such, Joshua
once considered his fortune to be the breath of life.
Although, not that opulence had always been. It took
years of hard work and avaricious pride; Caroline,
Joshua's mother, saw coming since Joshua was three.

He started selling homemade ice cream as part of the neighborhood's summer yard sales. By the age of six, Joshua, with the help of his parents, had established a four-hour weekend lemonade stand. After a few years selling lemonade, Joshua had earned enough to purchase a brand-new car, the year's latest model. And that was before obtaining his driver's license when he turned sixteen.

At twenty-three, a month after receiving an engineering degree, Joshua took a leap of faith. He started his own business, investing in real estate, while working full time at a research facility. A few years later, Joshua abandoned his civil engineering career, electing to focus more on commercial property ventures. With the help of a business partner, a robust economy, and flourishing housing market, needless to say, Joshua subsequently became a wealthy man. As his parents were growing older, Joshua felt compelled to keep a promise he had made to his mother, who wanted grandchildren. And so, Joshua kept his pledge. Before turning thirty, he married Dominique; a beautiful brunette with pearly eyes he had met at a banquet. Life was indeed a mirror of paradise. Joshua and Dominique had three children, including twin boy and girl, less than five years after getting married.

Thereafter, no one could explain what happened. Life seemed to have spun as though Joshua and his family were living inside a roller coaster. Tragedy struck, dreadfully awaiting a cure to help overcome life's ailments. *What is it?* What was it that turned everything   sour?

<u>2070</u>

The year, 2070, life has turned gloomy and intolerable. Love has grown cold. Joshua sits alone in a dark room. He has all the riches in the world. And yet there aren't enough tears to express his sorrows. Was it lack of sensible judgement in the pursuit of happiness? Joshua always thought of himself as being pragmatic. Divine wisdom, not luck, his parents reckoned had bolstered Joshua's rise to greatness. Life often never predicts a man's fall. Perhaps it is not such an irony that the luxuries of life allow abundant time to reflect.

"Oh my!

What has happened to me?"

Joshua cries out.

<u>2069</u>

The world has become numb.

The search for humanity is endless.

What's happened to love?

Seemingly gone with the wind.

"It is out of my hands," Lady Justice shells out.

Of course it is, Joshua gathers. The secret is out.

Long years and treasures have deceived true love.

"Sit"

"Eat"

"Where do we go next?"

The voices echo like pecking steel.

The world weeps of deafening solitude.

Joshua's soul reeks of emptiness.

<u>2068</u>

Dominique, Melody, and now Kathleen,

joy has come to taste bitter.

Its wings wallow as though they were the prey of a

hunter.

Kathleen was comparable to a first love.

How impetuous, yet cunningly shallow, her slayer.

Though the vows were not to be eternally honored,

darkness ensued without even as much a warning

So long, Kathleen

2067

The locust devoured her bones with haste.

Her eyes dimmed, nearing the tombstone.

Venomous!

It wasn't long before her frail flesh withered away.

When sickness eats at the one you love,

there is but *God* to pray.

Time isn't audacious enough in allowing a

bitter soul to repent.

Amen?

Too much of a burden, so little years.

<u>2066</u>

Nostalgia, in his life, was now a remittance

of unforeseen memories.

Joshua vowed not to lament.

Love could not have foretold the discontentment of
life,

soon to betray.

The appetite for forbidden flesh, buried long ago,

singed as though eager to everlastingly condemn.

Remorse overwhelmed like a slaughterer of nights.

The forever devoted and abiding heart wasn't at all

faultless.

<u>2065</u>

So temperate was love in the prime of life.

Never too young, yet never too old.

It blossomed in the vineyard of a man's heart.

The ballads of dawn were coveted more than the

most prized jewels.

Who knows love?

Who cherishes love enough, afraid to one day wake

up, and grieve in the bitterness of its waning gaze.

<u>2064</u>

It took a number of years.

Certainly makes one wonder,

why bestow such a gift, only to suddenly renege.

When a part of a man, so revered within himself,

slowly dies out,

what remains is all but a whisker of hope.

<u>2063</u>

Who would willfully relinquish such a thrill,
feeling on top of the world?
There were never any dishonest gains.
"By the sweat of a man's labor," Joshua's parents
taught him. It had also come to mean
— through the tears of a man's heart.

2062

Joshua had a strange dream;

the sign of the Cross etched in blood on his back.

When he got up, his chest was carved with red ink.

It happened the day after Joshua had returned from

a lengthy escapade around the world.

He thought, perhaps, it was portending his end.

Neither Joshua, nor Kathleen, could make sense of

the menacing occurrence.

<u>2061</u>

Foresight is the most judicious armor against
unpredictable winds.
It is liken to preemptive warfare, conquering the
boundaries of psychological veneer.
And yet, to Joshua,
Its ruse might as well had been rooted in modesty.
What was and always had been sovereign ruler of
his achievements was nearing its end.

<u>2060</u>

"It wasn't that long ago, love blossomed.
It still feels like yesterday.
I nearly ran out of breaths, but there you were,
poised with majestic beauty and virtue, which handed me
the key back to life.
Everything about you is graceful and incomparable.
You are, unquestionably, second to none my darling."
Joshua wrote to Kathleen on their tenth year
wedding anniversary.

<u>2059</u>

It is certain he had never been to paradise.
Yet when one awakes in the morning surrounded
by petals and roses, even for a man like Joshua,
it stirs the heart.
The sun veered just in time,
illuminating her well-proportioned curves.
His shoulders burned in her sweat.
It had all come back.

2058

Why fight true love?

Is it not the envy of most hearts?

Life ceases to exist when it's out of reach.

It was tragic, thinking of its cadence as familiar.

While Kathleen had a different rhythm,

her pulse reeked of a once revered scent.

However, she was different.

Kathleen was unlike the harlot and her scourge.

Her love was distinct and virtuously familiar.

<u>2057</u>

It could have been a wave of internal struggles,
Joshua led himself to believe.
Love felt nothing like what was once esteemed.
Betrayal is never transparent.
It left scars.
Some obvious, others hidden behind broken smiles.
Joshua could only hope time would heal the
wounds.
His infidelity was far reaching, beyond the
acceptance of forgiveness.
How would he comfort Kathleen's anguish?
What if she walks away?

2056

Perhaps, it wasn't enough, showering Kathleen
with flowers and diamonds.
A woman aching to love would undoubtedly want
more.
What man, nonetheless, would be gratified with
reprisal or pity to amend transgressions.
For even the most wicked of hearts fears the
reproach of the one it loves.

<u>2055</u>

Each had their own sweetened niche.
What was stolen in secret would soon taste acidic.
Wild hips had spoiled a welcoming treat
from a woman already in doubt.
Kathleen, assuredly, detected her husband's lack
of candor years earlier.
Marital infidelity, hushed in self-denial,
ravaged the noble wife from within.

2054

Elise

She turned out to be more than a shoulder to cry on.

One last time, he'd swore.

Where else would he find comfort,

if not in the delight of her breasts?

Joshua lifted his head, breathless.

Her perfume reminded him of summer.

She thrusted his head back, her chest engraved.

One last time.

Joshua's tears felt cold on her skin.

This time, it was finally over.

2053

There was a drop-down fan and a single
recessed lighting above each table.
Quite a strange assortment of ceiling features.
Out in the hallway,
colorful beams of florescent lights kindled the
wine cellar.
Joshua reluctantly sat on the oak bench facing the
staircase.
He would get a whiff before opening his eyes.
Hence, heightened the thrill of who it was going to
be each night.
It was part of the game they liked to play.
Joshua had promised to put an end to the lascivious
escapades
Who can resist such exotic rush?

2052

Marie-Anne

It was always at twilight, restless souls eagerly

tussled, seeking comfort under the cover of night.

"Hurry! Lie with me between the sheets," he'd

summoned a jaded lover.

"Surely, I will be the one," She reckoned.

Love, fleetingly in search of erotic meadows, seldom

forsakes home, Joshua thought to himself.

When it does go off course, it might not have no other

choice but to pretend it'll stay.

2051

It was his first time ever.

Somewhat rare for a man of his stature;

the once faithful socialite had suggested.

Of course, she as well surrendered, following many

episodes of wet pillows and sleepless nights.

It would be the reincarnation of love lost.

Joshua's sudden exuberance made it fair to surmise,

perhaps he wasn't fleeing a shadow of doubts.

<u>2050</u>

The days weren't so unfamiliar.
In fact, they were eerily comparable to the bouts of
disquieted rancor Joshua grieved over,
year after year.
The betrayed heart could only hope not to lose
itself in self-pity.
"Till death do us part," was as delightful as hearing
the morning songs of birds.
What would seem heartless to most, canvassing
debased pleasure, was to Joshua a symptom of an
artful crusade.

<u>2049</u>

Contemporaneous Love

There was finally joy, unadulterated bliss.

The heart shattered, blossomed, once more.

The wind sang a new song.

She was infectious, in whom resurrected love.

Her eyes were like the stars at moon light.

"I do" they both whispered.

It would be a new season, as they walked alongside

each other like doves.

<u>2048</u>

Oh what a relief!

Kathleen!

Daughter of an earthly king.

She was indeed one of a kind.

A love who shields and honors like Heaven,

no matter how much it rains.

<u>2047</u>

Kathleen

How different could she be?

It was all the same to a man whose mind had been
parched and stained with dark thoughts.

It was unconscionable to think love could be so
painful.

Conceivably, it might have been the frantic pursuit
of happiness that wounded so dearly.

How would the broken heart learn to trust again?

2046

Sadly, it was one of the toughest lessons to learn midlife.
Freedom of a sound mind had proven to be more
valuable than riches.
Parsing the memory of anguish in the quiet room
was like living hell yet again.
Love built without margins of perfection.
And yet, decayed in an instant.

2045

False virtue

Lost, running on empty.

What is life?

Flawed by the enmity of love.

Joshua recalled the days when he and his parents

sat on the stilted benches.

It would have been pretentious to blame his

depleting wealth as culprit.

Some had even hinted it was callous,

ascribing a mental collapse to justify a vain

matrimony.

It was such a travesty that the utmost discerning of

hearts could not foresee the ruin of a beleaguered

spirit.

2044

Rarely, love doesn't burn.

It was so disheartening;

no one wanted to talk about it.

"Foolish!" Cynics muttered behind closed walls

She had once been a beacon of sunshine.

Her well of sweet vapor had enticed flocks of lovers

like a chamber of honeycomb.

Alas, her vagrant appeal robbed Joshua of much

more than his dignity.

It wasn't so inconceivable he would end up

forfeiting a large sum of his wealth.

<u>2043</u>

Melody

Her fragrance abounded with healing virtues.

A verdant soul was teaching Joshua how to love

again.

She knotted his pain.

The stroke of her fingers were like coercing hands

on a string.

Her love — emphatic, yet unscrupulous.

How mesmerizing it was, living life on the fringes

of humanity.

"Oh Melody,

You've expunged the memory of what used to be.

I can love again."

2042

Joshua's Lament

What is life?

In the end, isn't it merely years wasted,

hoping there is really a God to bring the desolate

days back to life?

No other family member could help Joshua carry

the burden.

No clergymen could help him weep or express his

grief.

Too much mourning had rendered his soul

hopeless.

On this day, Joshua wished his world would end.

<u>2041</u>

When is it ever enough?
Joshua wished his parents hadn't taught him so
little about faith.
The strain of distress was almost ungodly,
grieving their loss.
Within a year, they had both expired like dried up
leaves.
Joshua's father endured most of the torment.
Some pains are like a plague at death's calling.
His mother had long surrendered her flesh to the
unforgiving monster before closing her eyes.
Joshua wasted no time in emptying out the fish
bowl.
Carol died on Mother's Day.

<u>2040</u>

Dad

There are things the eyes couldn't care to witness.

The ears would rather be stricken with deafness to avoid hearing.

The mind struggles to erase it all from memory.

The bond between mother and son, it has been said, is an eternal phenomenon.

And yet, the bond between Joshua and his dad was without equal.

Who, but the creator of the universe, can predict how things will end.

<u>2039</u>

Mom

From her womb, he received the breath of life.

How much of himself he would have relinquished

to see her come back to life.

She, much like Joshua's father, had forgone her own

needs and given Joshua the most refine treasures,

which rivaled that of any loving parents.

Her absence tormented Joshua, day and night.

"I wish I had loved you more,"

Joshua cried out over her tomb.

<u>2038</u>

Bella

She would help him take off his shoes after a hard day at work.

On most weekends, Joshua struggled to keep a straight face, munching on her half-baked cupcakes.

It was hard to convince her she wasn't Joshua's favorite, arguing with her brother over birth order.

She was more than Daddy's little girl.

She was his princess.

She would rush to get him at the first sound of the bells, both running after the ice-cream truck.

Why such an end?

It seemed odd that an angel could be raptured into the light through chasm of darkness.

Joshua adored her. She was Daddy's princess.

<u>2037</u>

Jack

Who knows the heart of a prince, if not the heart
who anointed him as such?
Joshua, undoubtedly saw in his first born, a soul
who breathed fire— the heart of a lion's cub.
He would've led the way.
At five years old, he wanted to build houses,
he'd told his dad.
"I miss you.
I miss you, son."

2036

Austin

He was a lot different than his brother.

A warrior with a heart of dove.

The kind who is often misunderstood.

Silent, yet strong.

He would grow up to find himself.

It would take years before finally acquiescing to his thoughtful and noble heart.

Nevertheless, not before many broken pledges and tear drops.

Not before the world would come to grips with a man who, unreservedly, cares and loves.

"I miss you, too, son.

No parents should know what it feels like to lose a child."

<u>2035</u>

Dominique

"Oh Dominique, my tower of strength.

If ever there was a woman crafted to love infinitely,

you wear her name.

A thousand years together wouldn't have been

enough.

The Love of My Life, My Queen!

There will never be one like you.

My life, for your life, I had vowed.

Love has a cruel sense of humor.

It teases, draws you in, then spits you out of its

spiteful claws.

Flesh of My Flesh, My Beloved,

crying a river of tears has not gratified the empty

space inside of me.

I want to lie down with you, wherever you may be."

2034

Tragedy

"There are days, evil makes a mockery of us all.

It jabs and taunts with laughter.

There is a tingling, an empty thrust, and a
whirlwind of unease.

There is a day when the God and gods of the
universe are in a tug of war to impart justice,
however righteous or unholy.

Who exactly rules this world?"

<u>2033</u>

Day of Wrath

Something terrible has happened.

One could hear the smashing of steel echoing

through thick rimes over their bedroom windows.

Everyone held their breaths.

Chaos!

There was already utter darkness before nightfall.

Hearts withdrew like ebbs of sunset.

There were no survivors.

No willing mercy from the Miracle Worker.

"My world has ended."

<u>2032</u>

Letters to Dominique

I'm planning a great future for us.

One with lots of grandchildren, I hope.

Bella, of course, has assured me three of her own.

It frightens me to hear her talk about things she's

yet to know about.

Jack, surely, will follow where I lead.

Can't say the same for Austin.

He might someday turn out to be a priest.

Mom and Dad are fond of the idea.

Life is beautiful, only because you all are in it.

Love, everlasting.

Joshua.

<u>2031</u>

A lot of it, many seem to think, is luck or greed.

It is all instinctual, I tell them.

Blessed with such auspicious gift, it is unimaginable

one wouldn't at least attempt to get the better of

this world.

And yet, my goal isn't simply to self-indulge.

It pains me, seeing angry and sorrowful thoughts,

buried underneath placid smiles.

It carries a never-ending load.

I'm told, I'm one of a few, ever so selfless that is,

which you have affirmed.

I wish most of us could see through one another's

disguises. Then again, some would really be

overjoyed as tyrants, playing *gods*.

Goodnight, Dominique. Love, everlasting.

2030

If the scale is to maximize wealth,

we are well on our way.

So tell me, My Beloved;

how is it that with the bat of an eye,

we can connect to another world, miles away.

Yet still, we fail miserably when it comes to the

affairs of the heart.

With the flick of a switch, we travel farther than

anyone could have imagined.

I breathe over a screen, in an instant, another world

becomes part of me.

What is it all worth, if one day, it will all end?

Nature pushes us, we rave. It says we must.

Our duty, evidently, is to oblige.

For my part, it is more than solely survival of self

that motivates the need to accommodate vain wishes.

We seem not to want to disappoint striving endeavors.

Where does it end?

Will it all matter?

Love, everlasting.

Joshua

2070

End of the Road

What on God's earth has happened to us?

We've prayed for greener pastures, only to garner

intolerable wrath.

Although I have given it my all, I wish at times,

I was less committed.

Dominique, I had promised to lie down with,

a resolution which baffles the mind.

I shamelessly sought the antidote, wondering,

which one would be my bride.

I was stunned at what I discovered.

I'm compelled to ask, when our world ends,

what if it's true; what we've been conditioned to believe.

Have we done enough?

Naomie Dieudonne

THE

MUG

SHOP

140

THE MUG SHOP

KYLE: This old lady came in yesterday. There was something about her that robbed me the wrong way.

JEN: well, it's Christmas; people are often not themselves during the holidays. They're under so much stress.

KYLE: She paid for the mugs with coins. Who does that?

JEN: Who knows? Maybe she wanted to get rid of them. I do the same thing.

KYLE: Nah, this was somewhat different. After she had paid for everything, she looked at me straight in the eye and asked when was the last time I had gone to church. I don't know, I mean the whole thing made me feel uncomfortable.

JEN: Oh C'mon! Stop fussing. The poor lady is probably one of those religious people who appreciates Christmas for what it should really be about.

KYLE: It's just that when she said it, her eyes, they peered right through me as if she was staring at my soul.

JEN: Oh Really? *Smiling.*

KYLE: I don't care what you think, Jen. It's not funny.

JEN: Were you afraid?

KYLE: No! Of course not. I was not afraid. It's just that... I don't know.

JEN: What?

KYLE: She said something that spooked me. Oh, forget it.

JEN: Go ahead, tell me, Kyle. What happened? What did she say?

KYLE: All right....uh...as she was placing each coin on the counter, she said the weirdest thing. "These coins have helped saved many lives," she said. It kind of freaked me out. I hadn't a clue what she was talking about.

JEN: Interesting. Did you ask her?

KYLE: What? What do you mean?

JEN: Did you ask her what did she mean about the coins?

KYLE: No, I thought it was best to leave it alone. And honestly, she couldn't leave fast enough after she spooked me out.

JEN: You shouldn't worry about it so much then. She could be one of those people who help feed the homeless.

KYLE: You know what's even more peculiar? She had me thinking about all sorts of things.

JEN: Like what?

KYLE: Let me ask you something, why do people go to church?

JEN: Um…I don't know, Kyle. They just go; I guess, to be closer to God.

KYLE: Sorry, forget it. I'm asking the wrong person.

JEN: What! I'm not an evil witch you know. If it's what you're trying to hint at. I go to church every Sundays, which is why I've asked for the weekends off.

KYLE: You do?

JEN: Of course, see, that shows how much you know about me.

KYLE: I see, well, I don't know. I was just asking. I would love to, maybe not. Anyway, tell me, why do you go to church? I've heard most people go to clean up their souls. I don't know if it's true.

JEN: One thing I can tell you, Kyle, I'm a lot happier when I'm at church.

KYLE: If you don't mind me asking, what kind of church do you go to?

JEN: It's non-denominational.

KYLE: Is that Christian? I mean, we've been working together close to a year; I've never heard you talk about church.

JEN: I guess I should have. People look at me a lot different when I tell them.

KYLE: Wow, so you're Christian? I had no idea. But why are you afraid to talk about your religion?

JEN: I don't like being judged.

KYLE: How? It's not like you're going to get beaten or stoned.

KYLE: Jen, did you hear me? Okay, that wasn't so funny.

JEN: Kyle, there are many parts of the world, where religion matters much more than you think. Take my family for example, we're far from the norm. My parents are Christians, but

Uncle Lou, Mom's brother, he's Muslim. We get along fine, but that's not always the case, Mom tells me.

KYLE: I see. Kind of makes it difficult for everyone at family events, I'm guessing?

JEN: Not really. We all love Uncle Lou. He's a nice guy. He respects our faith; we respect his.

KYLE: My parents used to force me to go to church when I was much younger. Now that I'm eighteen, they don't care if I go. I think my parents have been angry with God since my little brother died.

JEN: I'm sorry to hear that. How old was he?

KYLE: Less than a year old. He died in his sleep. My parents had been waiting a long time for another child. It got so bad, it drove Dad to have an affair. At least that's what he says. He felt Mom had blamed him for my brother's death.

JEN: How so?

KYLE: Dad was the last one to check on him. Mom was at work. She thought Dad had been drinking again.

JEN: Did you cry?

KYLE: I'm not sure if you can call it crying. I was numb. I didn't know how to feel. It's been about three years. Mom seems fine. Dad, not so much. You can't ever tell.

JEN: Well, I tell you what, pray for them.

KYLE: Pray? I'm not sure I remember how to do that.

JEN: It's almost the end of our shift. Do you think Phillip will be back tonight?

KYLE: He allowed me to close early over the weekend. He's not been feeling well.

JEN: I've heard, it probably has something to do with his mother dying a few years ago. It was right before Christmas season. She checked out while working in the store. From what I hear, he's not gotten over it.

KYLE: I hope he closes the shop next weekend. I would prefer not to be here on Christmas Eve. He hasn't said if he will.

JEN: Patrice says Phillip will most likely be at church. That's how he would like to spend the evening before Christmas.

KYLE: If he's not going to be here, he can expect me to stay home.

KYLE: Hey Jen, about this church thing. No matter where one goes to church, at the end of the day, aren't we all going to the same place?

JEN: It's kind of complicated.

KYLE: I know, right? As a Christian, isn't it all about this forgiveness thing?

JEN: Yes, but still a little more complicated. It's hard to explain.

KYLE: Isn't it about Jesus? He was born on Christmas Day.

JEN: Kyle! You're asking a lot of questions for someone who claims not to be that interested in church.

KYLE: I never said I wasn't. I just haven't gone in a while.

JEN: Forgive me. I hope I didn't offend you?

KYLE: Jen, can I ask you something? No....I mean…uh…Can I trust you with a secret?

JEN: Sure, what is it, Kyle?

KYLE: The day my brother died, I was in my room. I thought I heard him crying before Dad got to him. It could've been all in my head; I was too busy playing video games. I lied to Mom. I told her I was asleep. Do you think God will ever forgive me?

JEN: My goodness, Kyle! Am I the only one you've told about this?

KYLE: Pretty much. I probably will go to Hell, right?

JEN: No! Kyle, not for that! You didn't do anything wrong. God loves you; He really loves you, Kyle.

KYLE: Oh my God! Jen! She's here. Here comes that old lady again.

JEN: Where? I don't see anybody.

KYLE: She's walking towards the counter. Jen, Look, look!

JEN: Kyle, you're scaring me. The store is empty. There's no one here.

KYLE: She's here, Jen; she's here. She's talking to me.

JEN: Kyle, stop! What are you hearing?

KYLE: "Are the pieces of silver not good enough for you?"

KYLE: She was just here, Jen. I swear; she was just here.   She's   gone   now.

OTHER BOOKS BY NAOMIE DIEUDONNE

Tell Tale
A Book of Poetry

The Flower of Hope

www.ingramcontent.com/pod-product-compliance
Lightning Source LLC
LaVergne TN
LVHW021454080426
835509LV00018B/2286